Situational Meditation

Theory and Practice

ESTELLA CHAVOUS, Ed.D.

JACINTA CHAVOUS KAMBACH, Ed.D.

DocUmeant *Publishing*
244 5th Avenue
Suite G-200
NY, NY 10001
646-233-4366
www.DocUmeantPublishing.com

Published by
DocUmeant Publishing
244 5th Avenue, Suite G-200
NY, NY 10001

646-233-4366

All Scripture quotations marked "KJV" are taken from the Holy Bible, King James Version, Cambridge, 1769.

Editor: Anne C. Jacob, Popin Edits

Cover & illustrations by: Natalia Kambach

Asst Cover, layout and design by: Ginger Marks, DocUmeant Designs www.DocUmeantDesings.com

Library of Congress Cataloging-in-Publication Data

Names: Chavous, Estella, 1957- author | Chavous Kambach, Jacinta
      author
Title: Situational meditation : theory and practice / Estella Chavous,
      EdD,
   Jacinta Chavous Kambach, EdD .
Description: NY, NY : DocUmeant Publishing, [2025] | Includes
   bibliographical references.
Identifiers: LCCN 2025001305 (print) | LCCN 2025001306 (ebook) |
      ISBN
   9781957832609 paperback | ISBN 9781957832616 epub
Subjects: LCSH: Meditation
Classification: LCC BL627 .C493 2025 (print) | LCC BL627 (ebook) |
      DDC
   158.1/2--dc23/eng/20250425
LC record available at https://lccn.loc.gov/2025001305
LC ebook record available at https://lccn.loc.gov/2025001306

To God and our family, without you, we would not be where we are today. Thank you for your unwavering support. This meditation is for you.

Dr. Estella Chavous and
Dr. Jacinta Chavous-Kambach

CONTENTS

Preface

MANY PEOPLE AVOID MEDITATION due to its perceived religious associations. However, in the twenty-first century, meditation is increasingly recognized for its practical benefits in mental and emotional well-being, stress relief, and positive brain chemistry changes. These benefits are so significant that meditation is often completely disconnected from its religious roots in Western culture.

It's crucial to understand that meditation is not necessarily tied to any specific religion, but is an inclusive practice. Individuals and groups from all religious or non-religious backgrounds can incorporate meditation into their well-being.

Based on research completed by Dr. Estella Chavous and Dr. Jacinta Chavous-Kambach, this guide encourages you to view meditation primarily for its health benefits and as an integral part of your daily stress management routine, regardless of your faith or lack thereof.

This book offers straightforward overviews of the theory and practice of several common meditation types. Its goal is to empower you to make informed choices about your meditation practices based on sound research and your desired outcomes. In essence, *Situational Meditation: A Guide to the Theory and Practice of Meditation* equips you with the knowledge and tools to design your meditation routine, one that can hold whatever significance you choose in your life, whether it's for health and wellness, faith-based reasons, or any other purpose.

Introduction

SITUATIONAL MEDITATION: A GUIDE to the Theory and Practice of Meditation will share the history, origin, and benefits of the common forms of meditation. It will provide an introduction to meditation, revealing its overarching healing properties. This book also has two special chapters: one researched by Dr. Estella Chavous on special populations, particularly women, and the other researched by Dr. Jacinta Kambach-Chavous on meditation and music.

Each reader must understand the art of meditation's past and present practices to be informed about it. This book is not intended to state findings as facts or give readers all they need to know about meditation; it is intended to give each reader an introduction to the existing research and current practices, enabling them to select the best meditation form for them.

Inside *Situational Meditation,* you'll find an overview of the most common forms of meditation, an applicable GROUND change model, and an introduction to the *Situational Meditation Journal,* which will help you apply all that you learn and continue to learn throughout your journey in meditation.

Editor's Note

Situational Meditation: A Guide to the Theory and Practice of Meditation consists of extensive research into meditation, plenty of practical applications, and personal stories. As a result, Chapters 5 and 6 of this book contain scientific and medical jargon. This jargon is necessary to establish the credibility of the authors' extensive research into meditation. The authors are not merely presenting their opinions about meditation; they have thoroughly investigated much literature on the topic.

As is standard with all academic writing in the social sciences, in-text citations and references are generally written according to the American Psychological Association (APA) format. The APA style was created in 1929 by a group of psychologists, anthropologists, and business managers. The guidelines are updated periodically, with the most recent edition being the 7th Edition, published in October 2019. Here is a link to 7th generation APA writing (https://apastyle.apa.org/about-apa-style). Chapters 5 and 6 contain scientific and medical jargon that will thoroughly delight readers interested in this extensive research level.

However, if you are not interested in this kind of jargon, please do not pass on *Situational Meditation: A Guide to the Theory and Practice of Meditation*. The practical applications of how to meditate in Chapter 7, the authors' model of meditation in Chapters 8, and the powerful, personal stories of the effects of meditation throughout, are not just stories, but powerful tools that can inspire transformation and hope in your meditation journey.

Chapter 1: History of Meditation

THERE HAS BEEN MUCH reluctance to practice meditation due to all the preconceived notions and, frankly, needing to know the history behind it. Just as there are diverse beliefs about the origin of humankind, meditation practices also span a broad spectrum in their mental representation.

A practice rooted in spirituality has evolved to include approaches that train the mind, much like an athlete's training. However, no matter its origin, what remains constant is the universal therapeutic benefits that meditation offers. This enduring aspect of meditation is reassuring and inclusive, highlighting its resilience and adaptability for all, empowering individuals to take control of their well-being.

But where did this practice originate?

The answer is a journey through time and culture, with many diverse origins and forms of meditation, most of which began with religious, spiritual, or cultural roots. The origins of meditation can be traced back to ancient times, with some suggesting that even primitive humankind used meditative states while gazing into the flames of fire. As early as 500 BC, Buddha's art depicted him in meditation, a practice that would spread throughout Asia. The opening lines of the *Dhammapada,* spoken by Gotama Buddha 2,500 years ago, serve as a timeless illustration of the central theme of Buddhist teaching of the human mind in a series of mental exercises or meditations designed to uncover and cure our psychic aberrations.

Other countries have also adopted forms of meditation rooted in the Hindu-based Eastern style. Hindu meditation, a calming and reassuring practice, is a relaxed, contemplative moment focused on the present. This reflective moment, free of all thought, is not just a pause in the day, but a powerful tool for personal transformation. It opens the practitioner to spiritual enlightenment and the transformation of attitudes, instilling a profound sense of inspiration and motivation. As you delve deep into your being, you find your strength. This strength is believed to sustain the meditator throughout the day, preserving the calm center from being disturbed. Fear, doubt, and other earthly troubles are believed to be unable to touch the practitioner of Hindu meditation who has tapped into this strength.

Ancient Jews also practiced meditation. The Old Testament of the Bible references meditation in many of its chapters. As one example, Joshua, who succeeded Moses as God's chosen leader, spoke on the teaching of God in Joshua 1:8, saying, "This book of the law shall not depart out of thy mouth, but thou shalt meditate therein day and night, that thou mayest observe to do according to all that is written," (King James Version). The reference to meditate on what is written directed Jews of that time to stay keenly focused on the word given to them in the scripture to live a life in the direction of God.

As these examples illustrate, meditation has thousands of years of history and is primarily rooted in religion and spirituality. However, despite its ancient roots in these areas, its evolution into a science designed to explore its health advantages should encourage all to partake in its benefits, whether for religious reasons or otherwise. The body of research on meditation has found it to have positive mental and physical benefits, linking it to better overall health and an improved quality of life. No matter the form of meditation, its positive benefits have been attested throughout all practices in numerous cultures and religions, serving as a powerful motivation for all to incorporate it into their lives.

Chapter 2: Conceptions and Misconceptions about Meditation

THROUGHOUT HISTORY, A RICH tapestry of perspectives on meditation has emerged, each offering a unique insight into the human experience. These diverse viewpoints have influenced belief systems and broadened our understanding of what meditation is or isn't. In our quest to learn the history of the practice and how it affects individuals firsthand, we decided to research meditation on our own, through our experiences and those of others.

This idea to research the practical application of mediation came to us while working on getting our doctorates and learning about organizational leadership. We found it interesting that many leaders and their subordinates experienced burnout, depression, and health-related issues. We too, were suffering from stress during this journey and working to find ways to eliminate it. We decided to attend a mediation class and were surprised how simple focus could take our minds away from all the things we needed to do to complete our coursework. Knowing that writing a dissertation was the critical part of the doctoral degree, we were determined not to be counted among the many students who develop writer's block, burn out, and don't finish. We resolved to follow the process through to completion.

Upon entering the dissertation phase of the doctoral process, we began to pick up the practice of meditation and found that writing was more manageable when we took time to focus, clear our minds, and be in the moment, relieving stress and burnout. For instance, we experienced significant relief in mindful walks, deep breathing, and check-ins with ourselves, eliminating the stress and burnout we had experienced before the practice. This led us to think about looking beyond the organizational structures of leadership to look at the people structure and how simple time-outs and meditation benefited others and their well-being.

Our comprehensive research, which thoroughly examined the effects of meditation on a subset of individuals, the barriers to starting the practice, and the outcomes of those who experienced it, has unveiled a spectrum of perspectives on the meditation experience or lack thereof. We have identified various environmental conditions that can hinder or foster the practice, providing practitioners with a robust set of findings to guide their work.

By delving into the common barriers that deter individuals from engaging in the practice and the successes that inspire those who have embraced it, we aim to provide a comprehensive understanding of meditation that will captivate and inform our readers.

DEEP DIVE INTO THE BARRIERS

In conducting our research, we found that meditation has practical implications for those introduced to it. Time and complexity, belief structure, and personality type were the three most significant barriers to starting a meditation practice. These barriers and forms of energy can be managed and understood, as you will see as we delve into these three practical implications in more detail below.

"Meditation takes too much time, and I don't have time for a laundry list of to-dos: breathing, posture, and mind state."

There is some truth to this hindrance: meditation is about breathing, posture, and state of mind. When instructed to practice meditation, we are asked to prepare for the practice, which requires direction on certain things. But is this a bad thing?

The laundry list of things to do helps improve us physically, mentally, and spiritually. It boils down to communication and making the complex simple. All instruction depends on how it is communicated. If clear and concise, the instructions are easy to follow. Communication complexity happens when the amount of communication required to complete the instruction or achieve an objective is not precise or well-received. There are many choices in a meditation guide and how you practice, so choosing a practice that is easy to follow is just like choosing your favorite grocery store. To resolve this, we need to tap into the excellent apps, online tools, and resources to help us find the practice and guide that resonates with our communication style.

"Meditation is not of my faith or belief structure."

The second hindrance is a good reason not to practice meditation because a belief system and one's faith are the foundation of who we are. Remember that a foundational belief does not depend on other beliefs for justification, but makes one's belief personal. Does the practice of meditation require an implicit belief? Traditionally, meditation is strongly connected to religion, but today, it is practiced without a religious purpose. For instance, meditation is widely thought to be just an Eastern practice, but even Christians, by the fourth century, came to be called the *Desert Fathers*, who had sought to praise God in forms of monastic living. This adaptability of meditation to different belief systems is a testament to its inclusivity. Meditation is all-inclusive and designed to expand one's consciousness in differing practices. It is important to remember that belief systems influence how we perceive the world around us and the values we accept or reject. Designing to practice or not practice meditation takes discernment over perception. We should use this same discernment when choosing the menu of options available for meditative practice.

"Meditation is too difficult for me because my 'A' personality wouldn't allow me to do it right."

The last hindrance to practicing meditation is personality type. Unsurprisingly, this is a concern as it is a massive factor in how one participates in activities and cultivates relationships. With over 23 scientifically validated personality test assessments, personality plays a significant role in how we interact and act. Interestingly, studies found one form of meditation, mindfulness, to be considered a personality trait in addition to practice. Other studies found that meditation is strongly associated with flexible responses to stimuli, increased subjective well-being, and reduced psychological and physiological symptoms. So, if you are concerned with meditation being linked to personality, remember the numerous benefits of meditation and consider exploring mindfulness as a practice. Research also finds that meditation is linked to higher levels of extraversion and openness to experience and lower levels of neuroticism. The thing to realize is that no matter your personality style, studies show that the longer people practice meditation, the more their personalities change. This change, leading to personal growth and a better, healthier lifestyle, is a powerful motivator to overcome the hindrance of personality type.

Overall results from the deep dive of barriers to Meditation

This deep dive into participants' behavior barriers uncovered their perceived thoughts on meditation before they committed to practicing it. In addition to supplying their perception, we shared the reasons behind this perception and how it could change with more education and better interpretation. After all, perception is how something is regarded, understood, or interpreted, which could change with a concerted effort by demonstrating the positive effects of the change or, in this case, the meditation practice. This part of the research is essential, as it outlines how we see meditation from the outside looking in. It was interesting to see how our perspective changed after we experienced the practice of meditation, as did others who delved into it with more exploration.

Now, let's continue our research and examine those who have tried meditation and who we found to have tremendously different comments. From this subset of the research, after meditation, these individuals felt they experienced an increase in health, self-awareness/self-reflection, faith, and purpose. These positive effects of meditation should instill a sense of hope and optimism in those who are considering overcoming the barriers to practice.

DEEP DIVE INTO THE EXPERIENCE

"Meditation has saved my life and improved my overall health."

Anxiety, stress, and bouts of depression are the most prevalent conditions leading to poor health. Struggling with these conditions is a big part of our world. It is well documented that meditation improves these conditions, thus affecting overall health. The fact that meditation is a tangible and manageable task teaches us to let go of negative thoughts that don't serve us and enter into a calm state, improving overall health and well-being.

"Meditation has helped with my self-awareness and self-reflection."

Self-awareness is the ability to focus on yourself and your actions, thoughts, or emotions. It involves experiencing oneself so you know all aspects of yourself, including your traits, behaviors, and feelings. Awareness is the core of meditation, and it should help one see oneself and experience feelings, thoughts, and physical sensations more easily. Meditation permits you to be you; with this, you can better understand yourself and how to react to others.

"Meditation has brought me closer to my faith and my purpose in this world."

Belief systems help define us and take us through our journeys in life. How we interact with the environment, our families, education, and much more depends on our belief systems. These journeys involve moving from one place to another, leading us to our destined purpose. Our faith is a big part of defining our purpose. By quieting down our simple consciousness mind, we can better sit in silence and reflect, tapping into our faith. Because of this, it is not surprising that closeness to one's faith occurs in meditative practice.

OVERALL DEEP DIVE OF THE EXPERIENCE OF MEDITATION

The deep dive into the experience of meditation confirms the documented history and research on the positive effects it provides. Numerous scholarly studies on meditation support its positive effects on stress release and anxiety release, improve mental and physical health, decrease fatigue and insomnia, and provide an environment of peacefulness and calm. However, despite the research, testimonials, and miracles seen in its practice, there are still limits to its use due to misconceptions and lack of knowledge among those who perceive it to be a particular experience or way.

Ongoing Research

Our research on meditation is inclusive, involving diverse groups to ensure a comprehensive understanding and acceptance of meditation. By addressing various concerns, we aim to remove barriers and misconceptions, making meditation accessible to all.

In addition to the above research, the *Effects of Meditation Treatments in Managing Workforce Stress with Women in Leadership* focuses on special populations, particularly women in leadership, and how meditation can catalyze their personal and professional growth. *Situational Mediation* is a term we use to describe the application of meditation techniques in specific contexts, such as the corporate environment, to address unique challenges and enhance performance.

We all know that time is a precious commodity for women, especially those climbing the corporate ladder and juggling home commitments. Our research found that ten minutes a day of meditation was more beneficial than an hour for these women. This empowering revelation could inspire individuals, particularly women, to incorporate meditation into their daily routines. This study was just one population, women, but similar research on other populations has yielded similar results, suggesting that extended time is not a factor in the benefits seen.

One of the factors that may deter individuals from embracing meditation is the perceived time commitment required to learn the practice. However, our research, which included a diverse population practicing various forms of meditation for different durations, suggests that the learning curve is more about discipline and commitment than a specific skill set. The adaptability of meditation to different lifestyles ensures that anyone can reap its benefits, regardless of their daily commitments. These benefits, which include improved mental health and stress reduction, should inspire more people to explore the potential of meditation.

Another misconception about meditation is that it is exclusive to people of certain faiths or religions. While the history of meditation is indeed rooted in culture and religion, its use can be found in many beliefs, even to the extent that it may or may not be part of their doctrine and teaching. The evolution of meditative practice in Western culture has seen the development of secular forms of meditation, such as mindfulness, which are widely practiced in non-religious contexts. This inclusivity ensures that everyone, regardless of their religious beliefs, can benefit from the practice of meditation.

Meditation has transcended its traditional roots and become a brain science, with its benefits resulting in chemical and structural changes in the brain and body with regular use. A question that has raised concerns is if meditation creates a hypnotic state for those interested in the practice and whether one remains in control of the brain during the practice. According to the American Society of Clinical Hypnosis (ASCH), hypnosis is a state of inner absorption, concentration, and focused attention, enabling us to use our minds more powerfully. So, this definition would support meditation being a hypnotic state, but one we voluntarily put ourselves into when we focus on anything. This scientific understanding should reassure individuals that meditation is a well-researched and beneficial practice.

But is this state mind control?

A researcher named De Vol performed an interesting study that may unlock the answer. He studied Buddhist monks who meditated and Pentecostal Christians who used glossolalia prayer (a prayer in tongues that involves music, scripture reading, prayer, and meditation) to see if each group was still in control of their brains during both practices.

De Vol's study involved detailed brain scans and psychological assessments to compare the cognitive states of the two groups. While comparing the two, he found that the Buddhist monks remained in control of their brains. This study underscores the Empowering nature of meditation, suggesting that individuals in meditative states are in control of their minds, unlike what appeared to happen in the glossolalia prayer, which renders a person in an altered state of consciousness. This finding could open a new area of research for brain science, meditation, and glossolalia prayer.

Chapter 3: The Benefits of Meditation

"Active meditation exemplifies the life you long to live." —Paul Hines

THE SCIENCE OF MEDITATION yields several health benefits, ranging from enhanced memory power to increased creativity, stress reduction, and healing. Illnesses are huge stressors in life, which can be felt by the person who is sick and all those involved in their care. These illnesses can be acute or chronic, and they affect us emotionally, often taking a significant toll. Depression is a widespread reaction to sickness, and so is the development of negative behavior. In the story below, read how Tony dealt with the stress by using meditation to get him through his recently diagnosed cancer.

Tony was a very active and fit middle-aged man. He belonged to an elite fitness club in his area and used that facility to work out and socialize with his friends. To his friends, Tony was the picture of health. However, after being diagnosed with cancer, he fell out of his

fitness routine and hadn't been to the gym in a while. A few weeks before, his friends had started calling him and insisting on him meeting them. He decided to break the news to them and meet them at the juice bar at the gym.

It wasn't easy at the bar. Everyone commented that he looked even healthier and fitter even though he hadn't been to the gym. He usually would boast and tell them they needed to do a few more sets, but today, he had to tell them the bad news of his recent diagnosis of prostate cancer. It was very hard for him, mainly because he was, in their eyes, the picture of perfect health.

His friends were visibly shocked after he broke the news, their empathy palpable. They started to share their challenges with health in their lives and the lives of others they've known. These challenges experienced by others surprised him, and he felt sorry that he hadn't known about his friends' struggles earlier.

While in discussion, they shared their support for him, and one of them, recognizing his depressed state, invited him to a meditation class he was attending later in the day after their meeting. Meditation was 'out there' to Tony, but after more thought and persuasion from his friend, he decided to try it. At this point, he thought, 'Why not?' and agreed to join him.

Tony arrived at the class later that day and the meditation leader explained the principles of the class as he led them through a guided practice. In the class, he practiced breathwork, and there was no mention of spirituality, which he was not interested in. Tony felt this immense state of relaxation and mental and physical healing during the breathing cues. He even, at one point, forgot he was going through cancer at all. The session ended, which was only a 15-minute practice, which he hoped would continue more. The instructor shared a meditation CD and a pamphlet that contained the benefits, origins, beliefs, and evolutions of meditation after the class, all information that Tony had wanted answers to in the past.

Tony went through cancer therapy, and although it was not easy, he felt his side effects and the ability to get through them were easier with meditation. He is now on the road to good health, cancer-free, and back to where it was before his diagnosis. Tony has now added a routine that includes daily meditation and fitness workouts, and the results have been amazing for him. He can find that place of calm during stressful times and firmly believes that the stresses in his life, if maintained, would have prevented his sickness in the first place. He uses meditation regularly, adding it to his total well-being, a testament to the power of this practice.

As Tony's story demonstrates, active involvement in meditation can bring about transformative results, a fact substantiated by scientific studies. Tony's view of meditation as "out there" is a common misunderstanding, as is the confusion surrounding its selection process. Despite these misconceptions, there are numerous reasons to support meditation, with its many proven benefits being the most compelling.

Most agree that medicine should be more preventative than reactive, replacing bandages with cures. Because of this, the field of preventive and integrative medicine is growing. Research in preventive medicine has revealed that inflammation and stress are the root of most diseases, both of which can be managed. The human immune system drives the inflammatory process in disease, which is well established and gives us a beautiful opportunity to manage its effect on our bodies. Standard therapies suppress it but rarely work. However, alternative therapies have been found to turn off the response that causes inflammation, a response to cellular injury marked by redness, heat, and pain. Chronic inflammation has been seen in all types of conditions we are familiar with: asthma, peptic ulcers, tuberculosis, rheumatoid arthritis, chronic periodontitis, ulcerative colitis, chronic sinusitis, chronic active hepatitis, Alzheimer's, anemia, stroke, congestive heart and kidney failure, and more.

Stress also plays a vicious role in disease. It has been defined as a constellation of events consisting of a stressor precipitating a reaction in the brain that, in turn, activates physiological fight-or-flight systems in the body. Stress causes increases in cortisol and a host of inflammation triggers, such as diet, infections, and hormonal, metabolic, and neurological changes that break down in the gut. It is important to note that there is good and bad stress, each beginning with stressors.

Acute stress, commonly called good stress, is brief and short-term and has proven beneficial in creating motivation. Examples include starting a new job, giving a speech, meeting a deadline, or receiving criticism from a boss. Chronic stress, or bad stress, is more severe than good stress and has been associated with psychosis and physiological damage. Examples are financial hardship, family struggles, relationships, or work problems that are prolonged and repeat frequently over time.

We must find ways to manage stress, as psychological stress can significantly increase cortisol levels, influencing psychological and physiological parameters and ultimately impacting our health outcomes in sickness and disease. Meditation might serve as that wake-up call we need to motivate us to take action to manage our stress levels for better health.

THE BENEFITS OF MEDITATION

Meditation is a beacon of hope, offering relief for those dealing with inflammation, stress, disease, and weight loss.

The potential of meditation as a solution to the epidemic proportions of inflammation, stress, disease, and weight issues is undoubtedly intriguing and worth exploring. Research in mind-body therapies has practical implications that offer tangible psychological and health-functioning benefits, including reduced disease symptoms, improved coping with stress, behavior regulation, and improved quality of life and well-being. A good example of this is in the story of Taryn's weight loss journey.

Taryn had always struggled with being comfortable in her skin. She was overweight and for years had been having a difficult time getting the energy to make the change to a healthier lifestyle. Recently, apart from the physical consequences of obesity, she began to experience some mental consequences such as depression, low self-esteem, and body image disturbance, resulting in a lower quality of life. Her weight was affecting her mental and physical state. Fortunately, the one thing Taryn loved most was nature. Her love for nature inspired creativity, which she expressed through photography. This love for nature and her passion for capturing its beauty in her photographs inspired her to take walks on a nearby trail, where she could immerse herself in the natural world and find moments of peace and joy.

One beautiful September day, Taryn decided taking pictures by the nearby trail would be great. When she got on the trail, she saw three rabbits next to each other and began taking pictures. Taryn looked for a better angle and noticed the fourth rabbit eating aggressively, which was noticeably heavier than the rest. She looked at the heavier rabbit and thought, is that how I feel, isolated and alone? As Taryn continued to observe the rabbit struggle to keep up with the other, she realized how it reminded her of how hard it was for her to keep up with others and the sadness it was causing her. She knew it was time for a change.

Her sister was big into meditation and had been trying to get her to come, noticing the apparent depression and isolation Taryn was under. When she left the trail, she called her sister and broke down in tears, explaining how a rabbit in the forest was her reality in life. Her sister, always by her side, asked her to attend a mindful walking class with her. Taryn had never heard of mindful walking and wasn't even sure if she could keep up with the others. After learning how this group meets you where you are, Taryn decided to go. She met the group at the trail, nervous and not sure what to expect. The group had two designed guides, one leading people at different paces, leaving no one behind. The group walked silently, taking in the surrounding nature, which Taryn loved. She started with 5-minute walks and worked up to 10, 15, and 30 minutes three days a week. She even began to take her camera to capture the beautiful things in nature she loved. By the end of the month, Taryn had lost 13 lbs. and had the motivation to up her game on exercise and become a better person. She remembered her sister saying she used meditation and music to aid her toward a healthier lifestyle. Now, Taryn had for herself found a form of meditation that improved her physical and mental well-being, all thanks to the unwavering support of her sister.

The truth about weight is that everyone has beauty, regardless of size, until it affects their well-being. We are sometimes influenced by magazines, media, and social sites that promote looks and not what good health looks like, making it even harder for us to reach proper well-being. The journey to weight loss, weight gain, and mental health is not easy, but it is achievable with support, dedication, determination, and persistence. Taryn's story highlights how her journey led her to identify what she loved and couple that with focused meditation. You see, the benefits of meditation are situational, and it can be experienced in all you do: walking, eating, or in silence.

In this story, we showed how meditation, when practically applied, can significantly improve mental and physical well-being. This benefit can further be illustrated scientifically in the decreased expression of pro-inflammatory genes (RIPK2 and COX2) in the therapeutic use of mindfulness-based interventions. One study by Kaliman revealed a positive association between mind-body therapies and decreased C-reactive protein and other cellular inflammation marker levels in patients with type 2 diabetes, cancer, and cardiovascular disease risk factors, providing reassurance and confidence in the potential of meditation.

Pain management also significantly contributes to our health and ability to enjoy life. In 2011, researchers from MIT, Harvard, and Massachusetts General Hospital published a study in Brain Research Bulletin, which found that meditation training can improve a person's ability to control alpha brain waves, which minimize distractions. Subjects trained themselves to focus on physical sensations from certain parts of their bodies, leading researchers to believe that people who suffer from chronic conditions could train themselves to "turn down the volume" on pain, indicating meditation might be effective in pain relief.

Alternative interventions like meditation have demonstrated significant improvements in executive control, executive functioning, and increased emotional states such as heightened empathy, compassion, and resilience. Meditation fosters daily relationship harmony, enhancing self-control, communication, and openness. Despite the diverse effects of techniques, types, and styles, the intriguing idea that the mind can influence the body is gaining attention. The increasing use of meditation as an alternative intervention is a focus of research and mainstream holistic practices, empowering individuals to take control of their well-being.

Chapter 4: Types of Meditation and their Benefits

"This class is making me use my intelligence."
—Isabella Kambach (age 6)

IN SEPTEMBER 2015, ISABELLA, who was six years old, started first grade. We were excited about her first day and, like many families, couldn't wait to ask her about it. When asked how her first day at school went, she replied. "This class is making me use my intelligence." This statement stayed with us because a then-six-year-old observed the need for intelligence, which was a wake-up call. Her observation and statement helped us frame this chapter on choices of meditation and its benefits.

Meditation types are differentiated by being new, traditional, and individualized, and the benefit of each is questioned by the time spent practicing. As you embark on your meditation journey, you'll be amazed by the diverse range of options, each tailored to your beliefs. The key is to find a meditation style that resonates with you and promotes a sense of relaxation. Once you've found the right fit, you'll be able to enter a meditative state regardless of the situation or environment you're in.

It is crucial to also remember that meditation is a deeply personal journey that reflects your unique beliefs and foundation. Time spent in the practice is relative to the person, and some studies show that time spent in short periods resulted in an immediate increase in concentration abilities.

In the following pages, you will be introduced to the most common types of meditation. However, it's important to note that there are numerous other forms, each with its own benefits and practices. Your exploration should not be limited to the ones in this book. Instead, use this as a starting point to find a style and practice that resonates with you. The ones selected in this book were chosen because of the extensive research on their origins, goals, practices, and benefits, and their widespread practice in mainstream society.

CONTEMPLATIVE-CENTERING PRAYER EXPERIENCE

"The Trust for the Meditation Process embodies and promotes deep insight into the contemporary direction of social change. Its support of groups which give guidance into spiritual experience, not just spiritual talk, makes it a leader in its field." —Laurence Freeman OSB

Meditation Type: Contemplative-Centering Prayer

Origin: The historical roots of contemplative-centering prayer, as emphasized by Contemplative Outreach, are deeply embedded in Christian history. This form of contemplative prayer is a testament to the spiritual wisdom of the early Christians. First practiced and taught by the revered Desert Fathers of Egypt, Palestine, and Syria, practitioners also included St. Augustine and St. Gregory the Great in the west and Dionysius and the Hesychasts in the east. St. Gregory the Great succinctly described contemplative prayer as the knowledge of God, a divine gift that harmonizes the word in the scripture with the grace of God.

In the twentieth and twenty-first centuries, various religious orders, notably the Jesuits and Discalced Carmelites, initiated renewing their founders' contemplative orientation and sharing their spirituality with laypeople. The result was centering prayer based on Jesus's wisdom teaching in the Sermon on the Mount in Matthew 6:6 "When you pray, go to your inner room, close the door, and pray to your Father in secret. And your Father, who sees in secret, will repay you."

Goal: The belief underlying contemplative centering prayer is that oneness with God is not a goal to be achieved at will, but a profound transformation that occurs when one surrenders their entire being to God. This transformation leads to a divine union and a deep relationship with God. Contemplative-centering prayer meditation, based on Thomas Keating's teachings, offers a method to respond to God's initiative and the means to be fully present to God. It operates in grace, where the practitioner cooperates with the gift of God's presence.

Practice: Contemplative-centering prayer is a practice that involves sitting in silence for a set period with the intention of being present before God. During this time, one meditates on a sacred word. Catholic nuns provide evidence in support of the role of contemplative prayer and meditation in generating the joy and serenity that Jesus's allusion to the hidden treasure in Matthew 13:44 envisions. When used in centering prayer, mindfulness is "knowing what you do while doing it." Although the word *mindful* is used a few times in English translations of the Bible (ten times in the King James Version), the term could easily be substituted with a synonym like *attentive*. The construct of mindfulness is separate from Keating's teachings. However, he advocated contemplative-centering prayer as a way of growing into a state of tranquility, where one is less captivated by the opinions of others and more able to hear from God. The practice involves the ultimate union with God, a divine union, and a relationship with God.

Benefits: Contemplative-centering prayer meditation has been shown to literally *resculpt* our brains over time through contemplative spiritual practice and mindfulness meditation, helping us embrace the treasures of love, peace, and serenity even in these anxious times. Contemplative-centering prayer promotes the life skill of mindfulness. These benefits are theoretical and have been demonstrated through scientific research, offering a compelling reason to explore this spiritual practice.

The diagram on the next page summarizes the most common types of meditation. Its purpose is to not only introduce you to the origin, goal, and practice type, but to also help you understand that a universal platform of meditation can be practiced irrespective of your belief system. This illustration has been used along with the GROUND model as a reference.

Guided Meditation Experience

"Guided meditation is a voice inspired by your guide that opens you to love, truth, and a path toward revelations." —Estella Chavous

Meditation Type: Guided Meditation

Origin: The April edition of the History of Meditation informs us that guided meditation is gaining popularity, and its roots are in contemplative, Christian, Buddhist, and other traditions. In the twelfth century, Buddhist monks outlined steps to meditation—reading, pondering, praying, and contemplating—that form the foundation of all meditation practices. Whether you seek guidance in a group, from a mentor, or through intuitive self-discovery, the personal meditation journey inspires and motivates you to explore your inner self.

Goal: The goals of guided meditation are to clear the mind, facilitate relaxation, reduce stress, and enhance personal and spiritual growth. The spiritual aspect does not have to be emphasized for those who do not adhere to a particular faith; many use guided meditation focusing on improved health. A guide can use many techniques to induce the mind to a calm state, thereby reducing stress. Some forms fill the mind with positive imagery, affirmations, etc.

Practice: Guided meditation is often practiced with a recorded or in-person guide. As the sessions continue, the need for a guide decreases. The auditory guidance indicates imagery, imagines affirmations, and states peacefulness or imagined desired experiences. These guided states of consciousness focus on one's awareness and attention. A lot of concentration is focused on breathing and verbal instructions, which teach one to relax and clear the mind.

Benefits: *Intervention and Health*—Guided meditation has been commonly used in intervention, and its health benefits have been reported. Some of the leading health benefits are its combative effects on illness, its power in lowering hypertension, reducing the onset of asthma, allergies, and pain, and its *Increased relaxation*, creating a sense of balance. It also reduces depression, anxiety, and stress, all of which support increases in coping skills.

MINDFULNESS MEDITATION
EXPERIENCE
> "Happiness does not depend on what you have or who you are. It solely relies on what you think." —Buddha

Meditation Type: Mindfulness Meditation

Origin: The origin of mindfulness meditation is derived from ancient Buddhist and yoga practices. It is a mental state characterized by nonjudgmental awareness, teaching people to live each moment as it unfolds. It is a state of rigidity in which one adheres to a single perspective and acts automatically. When mindful, one is trapped in a rigid mindset and oblivious to context or perspective. Practitioners have adopted variations of this form of meditation specific to stress reduction. These nonreligious programs are anchored in the development of awareness in moment-to-moment experience.

Goal: The goal involves focusing on the present circumstances and accepting them without judgment. Mindfulness means paying attention in a particular way: on purpose, in the present moment, and non-judgmentally. Practitioners learn to be mindful and calm their minds.

Practice: This practice is an accepting and non-judgmental focus of one's attention on emotions, thoughts, and sensations. The focus is on an object (like breathing). Mindfulness represents a method of learning to relate directly to whatever is happening in one's life, a way of taking charge of one's life, a way of doing something for yourself that no one else can do for you-consciously and systematically working with your stress, pain, illness, and the challenges and demands of everyday life.

Benefits: The practical applications of mindfulness, as revealed by research conducted at Massachusetts General Hospital, are truly empowering. These studies have correlated mindfulness with changes in brain chemistry in individuals who participated in mindfulness-based stress reduction. Lazar's research further reinforces this, showing that practicing mindfulness meditation thickens the mid-prefrontal cortex mid-insular region. These changes in brain structure may underlie some of the cognitive and psychological improvements, indicating that people are not just feeling better because they are spending time relaxing.

The field of mindfulness research, rigorously explored over the last 30 years, continues to inspire hope. The latest research model created by Langer, whose constructs are more Western and scientific, and Kabat-zinn's, whose multifaceted construct is used more in clinical settings, has proven to help elevate positive psychological mind states, mitigate physical disorders, and improve aspects of well-being in both healthy and clinical patients. This underscores the benefit of using mindfulness to help alleviate pain, depression, anxiety, and stress, as well as in helping with coping skills.

CHRISTIAN PRAYER MEDITATION EXPERIENCE

"This book of the law shall not depart out of thy mouth, but thou shalt meditate therein day and night, that thou mayest observe to do according to all that is written therein: for then thou shalt make thy way prosperous, and then thou shalt have good success." —Joshua 1:8

Meditation Type: Christian Prayer Meditation

Origin: Genesis 1:1-3 tells us, "In the beginning God created the heaven and the earth. And the earth was without form, and void; and darkness was upon the face of the deep. And the Spirit of God moved upon the face of the waters. And God said, Let there be light: and there was light."

Christians often avoid meditation because they associate it with Eastern religions. However, the Christian Bible is filled with examples of meditation. For Christians, the Old Testament covers the beginning of the world, Israel's history, and God's law, and the New Testament documents Jesus Christ's ministry and how his actions saved the world.

In the Old Testament, there are two primary Hebrew words for meditation: Haga (הגה), which means to utter, groan, meditate, or ponder, and Sihach (שׂיח), which means to muse, rehearse in one's mind, or contemplate. These words can also be translated as dwell, diligently consider, and heed.

Goal: In the Bible, which is the word of God for Christians, the word "meditate" or the act of meditation is mentioned twenty times. Piper, wrote that the word of God inspires, informs, and incarnates. The word inspires Christians, meaning that the word commands Christians to pray, makes promises to Christians of what God will do if they pray, and tells stories of great men and women of prayer. Our thoughts determine our behavior, so what we think about is essential. That is why Christians believe God wants them to think about his word, which is the same thing as meditating on it. Meditation is *focused* thinking, so for Christians, the goal of meditative prayer is to focus on God's word so it can transform them into what God wants them to be.

Practice: The definition of meditation is to engage in contemplation or reflection. The word informs, meaning it tells Christians what to pray and itself becomes the content of prayer, and the word incarnates Christians, meaning that prayers are often invisible and concealed in the soul, the closet, and the church. Christian prayer concentrates on God's word to increase awareness of him and what he would have Christians do. To pray means to speak to God with adoration, confession, supplication, intercession, or thanksgiving. Meditation in the Christian form can be done with a guide who can lead you in biblical principles or the word or through silent contemplation on a sacred word, affirmation, or scripture—all done by turning the mind over to God and his word.

Benefit: One of God's goals for Christians is to build a relationship with Jesus Christ and to fill their minds with Christ's word so that Christians can help others (through acts of benevolence like feeding the poor, helping the homeless, visiting the incarcerated, etc.) and themselves (through gaining control of greed, anger, adulterous desires, etc.). In addition, James 5:16 says, *"The effective prayer of a righteous person can accomplish much."* The benefits are all coming and can be seen in mental, physical, and spiritual health miracles and in inner peace, self-growth, faith, awareness gained, and salvation.

TRANSCENDENTAL MEDITATION EXPERIENCE

"The thing about Meditation is: You become more and more you." —David Lynch

Meditation Type: Transcendental Meditation

Origin: The researcher Mason tells us that Transcendental Meditation was developed by Maharishi Mahesh Yogi in 1957, a famous Hindu Guru Swami Brahmananda Saraswati student, to develop the mind so that a person can rise above or "transcend" beyond the noise and stress of daily life. The origins of transcendental meditation began in the Far East and later spread to the Western world;

it is based on Vedic Meditation. Transcendental meditation is a relatively new form of meditation compared to yoga and Buddhist meditation.

Goal: While transcendental meditation is not affiliated with any religion, it did have a political association with the Natural Law Party. This party, formed in 1992, aimed to use the principles of meditation to address society's problems—crime, injustice, economics, and environmental issues. Maharishi Mahesh Yogi, the founder of Transcendental Meditation, tells us that its goal is to achieve a state of enlightenment. This enlightenment allows us to experience inner calmness and a quiet state of least excitation, even when we are dynamically busy.

Practice: Transcendental meditation is a simple technique and is not a philosophy. It is natural, simple, and effortless. It is designed to take the mind from active levels of thinking to a state of less mental activity, and its goal is to create inner peace and wellness. Hinduism concentrative (transcendental) meditation includes the categories of open awareness, guided practice, and mindfulness meditation. The principle behind the transcendental meditation technique is that the source of all thoughts is the deepest level of the subconscious and far beyond what the ordinary senses can experience. In this meditation, the practitioner takes one thought or sound and focuses on this so that it can be experienced in the deepest possible way. During Vedic Meditation, the body slows down at least as much as it does after a few hours of sleep. As a result, a lot of physical stress and the associated mental stress are released quite spontaneously and very quickly. We find rest for the body and rest for the mind.

Benefit

This meditation is a simple, natural process that enhances the balance of the physical nervous system by alternating profound restfulness with regular daily activity. It's important to understand that every physical activity has a corresponding mental activity and vice versa. This principle underscores the unity of body and mind in transcendental meditation, highlighting that they are not two separate entities but part of a unified whole that should always be in complete harmony. Concentrative meditation is the most common and used to treat occupational stress in many populations. Studies have shown its effectiveness in managing stress, anxiety, blood pressure, chronic pain, and insomnia. It also helps to reduce stress levels in the body, leading to overall good health, an increase in a person's creativity, a heightened intelligence level for the meditator, and self-realization. It can even help you live longer.

The diagram on the next page summarizes the most common types of meditation. Its purpose is to not only introduce you to the origin, goal, and practice type, but to also help you understand that a universal platform of meditation can be practiced irrespective of your belief system. This illustration has been used along with the G.R.O.U.N.D model as a reference.

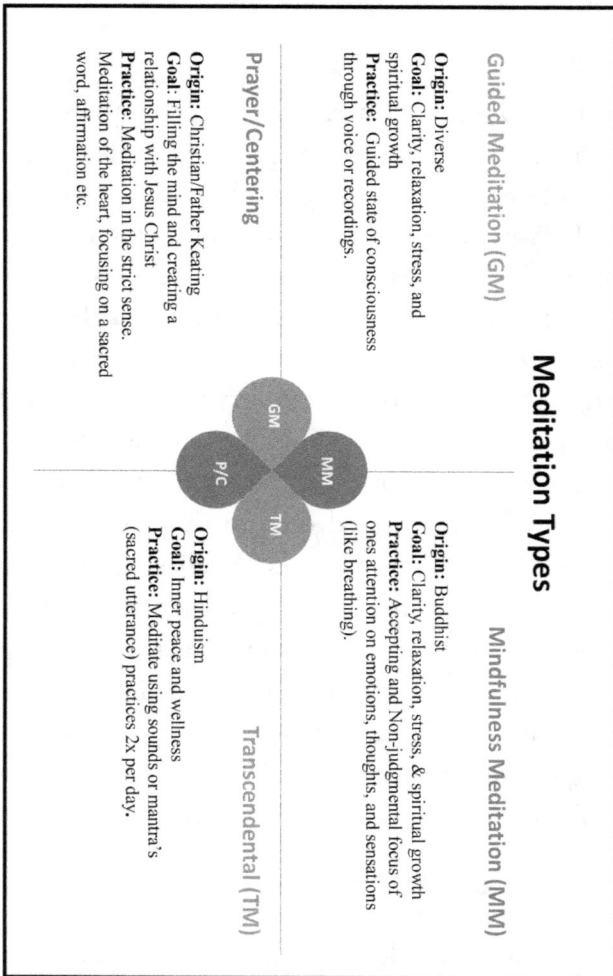

Meditation Types

Guided Meditation (GM)

Origin: Diverse
Goal: Clarity, relaxation, stress, and spiritual growth
Practice: Guided state of consciousness through voice or recordings.

Prayer/Centering

Origin: Christian/Father Keating
Goal: Filling the mind and creating a relationship with Jesus Christ
Practice: Meditation in the strict sense. Meditation of the heart, focusing on a sacred word, affirmation etc.

Mindfulness Meditation (MM)

Origin: Buddhist
Goal: Clarity, relaxation, stress, & spiritual growth
Practice: Accepting and Non-judgmental focus of ones attention on emotions, thoughts, and sensations (like breathing).

Transcendental (TM)

Origin: Hinduism
Goal: Inner peace and wellness
Practice: Meditate using sounds or mantra's (sacred utterance) practices 2x per day.

GM　MM
P/C　TM

Chapter 5: Meditation for Special Populations

"When I meditate, I win!" —Nickolas Kambach (age 3)

WOMEN IN THE WORKFORCE AND STUDENT STRESS

WHAT WORDS OF WISDOM from my three-year-old grandson: "When you meditate, you win!" Thankfully, his school stands out as one of the more progressive ones, employing meditation as a key tool to shape its students' behaviors.

Meditation, a powerful tool, has been proven to significantly impact the stress levels of women in the workforce and students. This chapter will focus on these populations, providing reassurance of meditation's proven positive impact. It will discuss the epidemic of stress and coping techniques, therapies, and treatments, and the empowerment that meditation provides to these populations.

Workforce Stress for Women

It is estimated that nearly one billion women in the world could enter the global economy during the coming decade and are poised to play significant roles in countries around the world. This entry into the workforce will have different concerns for employers specific to women. They will face unique obstacles that include discrimination, stereotyping, conflicting demands of marriage, and work/life and social isolation, all of which fuel stress-related concerns. Additionally, women in the workforce may be managed or working with a different generation, who must be aligned socially, technologically, and in experience. Listen to Kari's story, which illuminates the issue and shows how meditation helped her overcome her misfortune.

Kari spent most of her career in the same business. She was successful and good at what she did. However, Kari recently went through a huge shock when she was unexpectedly let go for a younger person with less experience who was more technology savvy. She was humiliated, angry, and hurt at first, but soon afterward, she began to feel the real fear that this loss of a job would throw her into financial turmoil. Depression and increased anxiety began to set in, especially around the uncertainty in her job future and lifestyle change.

Knowing her worth in the company, a younger former co-worker continually stayed in contact with Kari, as she had played a significant role in Kari's business journey. This co-worker, aware of Kari's stress, had been suggesting meditation to her for some time. Kari had consistently declined, citing various reasons. However, the continuous rain and cloudy skies in Seattle, which negatively influenced her mood, finally convinced her to try it. At this point, she was desperate to find a way out of the deepening depression she was feeling. It was taking a toll on her, so she forced herself that day to gain enough strength to make it to the community center's meditation class.

Feeling disempowered initially, she took part in the experience, which was scary, yet intriguing. As she continued, she felt a transformation from fear to empowerment, inspiring hope for a better future. The voice guided her to a place of calm that she knew but had forgotten about in the last few months. It was a place that always made her smile, and she felt that there wasn't a worry in the world. This place was, for her, a special place in Hawaii that she always reflected on when asked about good memories. After the session, many shared their experiences with the group, and she realized she was not alone. The sense of community in the group was palpable, and she found a place in her memory where she could always escape the mental challenges of life to find calm. She began to meditate 2-5 minutes a day and, in one month, had a new job and a newfound passion. She now meditates using a routine of 10 minutes a day with three other

members of that same meditation group, feeling con-
nected and supported.

EPIDEMIC OF STRESS (WORKFORCE)

Kari's story is not uncommon. A recent survey conducted by CareerBuilder showed that millennials
currently manage 35 percent of the US workforce,
making them the largest generation in the country's
history and the largest workforce demographic.
One issue that was found in the survey was that
young managers show a strong preference for hir-
ing other younger workers. This statistic can leave
older workers feeling alienated and squeezed out of
the workplace, causing stress and depression, as we
saw with Kari. This type of stress, real or perceived,
can be helped by using meditation. It is crucial to
note that choosing like-minded career individuals
happens regardless of age, race, or another identifier.
Therefore, it is imperative that we all work together
to raise awareness of employment issues with work
diversity and how to manage these issues with
meditation.

Research and real-world situations have shown that
women, often juggling work and family responsi-
bilities, face unique stressors in the workplace. The
resulting work/family conflict can lead to increased
stress and burnout. As they navigate the transition
from traditional to non-traditional roles, while also
meeting work demands, it becomes crucial to create

more flexibility in the workplace to cater to their specific needs.

Gender exclusion in organizations is a significant issue that has consequences, including impacts on health, for both men and women. Despite women's dominance in many labor forces, their numbers do not reflect their power. As we anticipate a significant shift with more women taking on leadership roles, it's crucial to work towards reducing the potential stress these high-potential women could face due to unclear promotional opportunities, glass-ceiling barriers, gender socialization differences, work-related discrimination, gender-role stereotyping, conflicting demands, and the likability test, a challenge that accomplished men don't often face.

Student Stress

This plight is not just for women; student stress is real. In school, 75 percent of high school students report experiencing boredom, anger, sadness, fear, and stress. The leading causes of stress are heavy workloads and lack of sleep. Discover how the practice of meditation, a powerful tool, helped support Jennifer's student stress during a difficult time.

Jennifer went to college late in life. She was a wife and a mother of three, with one child on the way. This last pregnancy was unexpected, and although it was a blessing, she felt it would result in her needing to take a break from school. The pressures had already started piling up, and she didn't know if she could keep up. Although supportive, her husband could not maintain the household alone. He was the leading provider, and they had established clearly defined roles, each contributing to sustaining the household.

The final days of the semester were approaching, and two primary assignments were due. These were also group projects, which required even more time. The first conference call with classmates established all the to-dos, and the next would be a run-through of all that was required. After the first call, she said, "to-dos and to quit." How would she make time for this when she was sick in the morning, taking kids to school, and preparing for the evening meals and activities? As organized as she was, she didn't think it could be done; mornings were when she did her best work. She began to feel herself fall into a panic and became depressed at the thought of what the outcome of all of this could be.

She started flipping through the radio channels and stumbled on an ad for a transcendental meditation class. She had heard how it helped develop focus and productivity and worked well for students, so she quickly called the number and registered for an upcoming class that, fortunately, started that week. She attended, learned the practice, and immediately began doing it daily. The results were nothing short of transformative. Her meditation routine not only helped her manage stress but also brought about a profound personal transformation. It gave her the strength and focus to get through the school session and be ready to take on more. It taught her to develop her mind so that a person can rise above or "transcend" beyond the noise and stress of daily life. She can't say enough about how transcendental meditation has changed her life, and she hopes her story can inspire others to find their own path to managing stress.

EPIDEMIC OF STRESS (STUDENT)

Academic problems like poor grades, inability to retain information, problems with teachers, inability to meet deadlines, and just plain overload of workload are familiar to students of all ages. In addition, stress, anxiety, and depression were all reported as top factors that negatively impact academic performance. A National College Health Assessment Report found that 55.5 percent of undergraduate and 57.1 percent of graduate students experienced more than average or tremendous stress in 2012. Furthermore, 6.1 percent of undergraduate and 4.4 percent of graduate students see a mental healthcare professional at their campus counseling services. Jennifer's story shows how the overall stress of student workload and balancing a home was managed through transcendental meditation.

Coping Techniques Therapies and Treatment

The brain controls how humans react to stress. Environmental stimuli that influence social and emotional behavior constantly influence the brain. Stress is natural and a part of us. However, it is not the stress but how we mitigate the stress triggers. To mitigate these stress triggers, some have advocated taking breaks, appreciation of yourself and family, strategic thinking, feeding your favorites, and embracing insanity, all elements of some meditation practices. The importance of reducing stress triggers cannot be overstated, and it is crucial that we all take a proactive approach to this. However, finding ways to institute treatment programs that maintain sustainable levels of stress reduction within workplaces can be problematic even with them being a common element in employee wellness programs. The challenge of implementing and delivering stress management programs for worksites and institutions is one that HR professionals, school administrators, and researchers are uniquely positioned to address. Recent workplace and institutional interventions, such as meditation, have shown promise in managing workplace and student stress, as demonstrated in our research on women in leadership and our meditation practice. These workplaces and educational institutions recognize the potential of meditation, prayer, yoga, somatic therapies, and biofeedback in managing disease symptoms and the underlying thoughts, feelings, and emotions that influence health.

Benefit of Meditation on Special Populations

Despite the challenges faced by women and students in the workforce and educational institutions, the use of meditation has shown promising results in alleviating stress. The substantial evidence supporting the benefits of meditation in reducing various medical ailments, including stress, offers hope for a healthier, more balanced future for these populations.

It's important to remember that stress is a universal experience, not limited to specific populations. While our research and meditation practice has focused on women and students, we believe everyone can benefit from meditation. The practice offers significant mental, emotional, and physical health benefits, fostering a sense of connection and support in our collective wellness journey.

Chapter 6: Meditation and Music Benefits

"Opening oneself to music and meditation can lead you to an enlightened self and a purpose- filled life." —Jacinta Ck

THE SCIENCE OF MUSIC

THERE IS LIMITED BUT intriguing literature on the use of music in organizations. While the literature on the use of music in organizations is limited, the potential benefits of using music for stress reduction are significant and should be noticed. Music, with its long history of use since the engineering revolution, is believed to possess favorable therapeutic properties. Emerging studies that measure music's impact on health and stress reduction are beginning to surface in the literature, offering hope for its potential in organizational settings. However, despite these promising findings, using music treatment for stress reduction remains an under explored option in many organizations.

Previous research has convincingly demonstrated that a balanced brain, characterized by balanced brainwaves, plays a critical role in promoting healthier living and enhancing productivity. The balance of brainwaves facilitates critical learning (left brain) and creativity (right brain), enlightening us about the potential for increased productivity in individuals who engage both sides of their brains.

Researcher David Csabai has introduced a stress intervention that utilizes brainwave entrainment, which uses *frequency-following responses.* These responses are the brain's natural tendency to sync with external stimuli, such as sound or light, and align the brain's internal processes with these stimuli. This can help remove or change unwanted behavior patterns and attitudes. The frequency-following responses can also assist with meditation affirmations and visualization of one's goals. Additionally, binaural beats *(brainwave audio)* can be used to achieve different mind states, leading to deep relaxation and meditation. They also greatly influence self-improvement and overall health.

Brainwave entrainment comprises four frequencies in which the brain's internal processes mirror external stimulus. Understanding these frequencies can make us more aware of our brain's functioning. The first frequency, alpha, is typically associated with a relaxed, peaceful state and operates between 8 and 13 cycles per second. It is experienced during daydreaming, fantasizing, and creative visualization.

The second, beta, is associated with our normal brain rhythm in a wakeful state, operating between 13 and 40 cycles per second. Beta is experienced when a person thinks, is alert, conscious, and is logical. The third, theta, represents the state in which we can access our subconscious and operate between 4 and 8 cycles per second, activated by dream sleep. Deep music, which results from this, is the brain state generally associated with creative thinking and allows us to tap into our inner genius. The last frequency is Delta, the lowest frequency, operating between 0.5 and 4 cycles per second. Delta frequencies are produced during deep sleep.

Music Treatments

Music therapists have focused on music's benefits and pragmatic uses, but rarely on healing. Music treatments, also called sound healing, are an alternative healing method that uses new-age music, opera, and classical music to soothe. According to Yehuda, there are three therapeutic functions attributed to music:

1. *Restoring the soul or body.*
2. *Creating the sensation of pleasure through movement.*
3. *Inducing releases that purge the soul of emotional conflict.*

So how does it work?

Earlier, we mentioned certain brain waves benefit you mentally and increase your creativity and focus. Here is how it works.

An article in *Modern + Mindful*, tells us that "When you hear two tones—one in each ear—slightly different in frequency, your brain processes a beat at the difference of the frequencies. This is called a binaural beat. Your brain, however, gradually falls into synchrony with the difference. While there are some rules regarding the frequency levels, binaural beats have been explored in music for tuning instruments, such as pianos and organs. What's truly intriguing is their potential health benefits, as shown in the studies above.

While it's clear that music can positively influence our biological system and therapeutic outcomes, there's still much to learn. More research is needed to fully understand the lasting effects and duration of these outcomes, sparking curiosity and engagement in this exciting field.

Benefits of Music

Decades of research show that meditation is an effective complementary therapy for health conditions such as high blood pressure, cancer symptoms, and chronic pain. It's also believed to improve mental health, lower stress, and contribute to an individual's holistic health and well-being.

Dr Michael H. Thaut and his team of researchers have established that neurologic music therapy is not just a theoretical concept but a scientifically proven method with evidence-based therapeutic techniques. These techniques have been shown to effectively retrain and re-educate brain and behavior functions in neurologic disorders and injuries, particularly in motor recovery after stroke. The neurologic improvements seen in the brain related to control movements, attention, speech production, learning, and memory are not mere observations but scientifically validated outcomes of music. Shannon K de l'Etolie and Blythe LaGasse's findings further reinforce the scientific basis of music therapy. They discovered that the brain areas used during music perception and production are not exclusive to music and that music learning can bring about significant changes in the brain. These findings have helped to identify the underlying scientific mechanisms for change, growth, and learning that can result from music therapy, providing a solid scientific foundation for its effectiveness.

As the research demonstrates, music possesses a transformative power to heal and aid individuals in coping with illnesses. It operates physically by inducing a state of transformative relaxation, which reduces stress levels and enhances cognitive function.

Music meditation, a practice that focuses on breathing while meditating and listening to music, is particularly effective in calming the mind and relaxing the nerve muscles, thereby reducing brain noise. A 2022 study found that sound meditation can reduce stress, tiredness, and negativity compared with silent meditation. Other studies have found that meditation and music listening can improve mood, sleep, and well-being in adults with cognitive decline. The research also highlights the intriguing potential of audio with binaural beats to enhance mental health and foster creativity and focus.

Chapter 7: How Do I Meditate?

"Let the things on earth I borrow create fruits for tomorrow." —Estella Chavous

KNOWING HOW TO MEDITATE and questioning the correct way is a frequent question meditation guides get asked. There is no wrong or right way to meditate, and this is partly due to the various beliefs about how to experience it. Success comes when you take responsibility for your learning and choose a practice that resonates with you. Regardless of the style chosen, the benefits of any meditation far outweigh the risks.

For those ready to embark on the meditation journey, we offer some practical considerations to kick-start the process and keep you engaged. Meditation is a lifestyle change, and the first step is to *GROUND* yourself for successful change. This process, while not complex, requires a commitment of mindset. Our *Chavous-Chavous-Kambach GROUND change model*, designed to guide you to success, is a straightforward tool. While there are various change models inspired by pioneers like Kurt Lewin and John Kotter, ours focuses on preparing your mind for the change that meditation brings.

Estella Chavous and Jacinta Chavous-Kambach created the *Chavous/Chavous-Kambach GROUND change model* as a comprehensive tool with six steps to prepare and support you for change.

1. *Getting acclimated to your environment*
2. *Realizing your vision*
3. *Opening your mental capacity*
4. *Using meditation to increase your inner strength*
5. *Noticing wins and conflicts*
6. *Dedicating yourself to continual change and renewal*

The model encourages you to observe each area, paving the way for successful change.

LEARNING TO AVOID DISTRACTIONS

As you have read in this book's *conceptions and misconceptions* chapter, finding the time for meditation can be challenging for some. Meditation sounds good, but how will I realistically avoid distractions when they occur?

One woman wrote to us:

My demanding boss, my addictive cell phone, and my busy, draining home life make me question whether this practice is right for me.

I am a single parent who continually experiences stressful days at work. I start at 7 a.m. and leave work at 3:30 p.m., just enough time to rush to pick up my children from school. I must stop and get a few groceries, which leaves me to arrive home at 5 p.m. I fix my kids a quick snack before preparing dinner, and we sit down to eat it at 6:30 p.m. By the time we're done eating, putting the food away, and doing the dishes, it's 7:30. I remember committing to my practice and hurrying to my room at 7:45 to meditate for ten minutes. But 4 minutes into my meditation, one of my children knocks on the door. I have less than the planned ten minutes, and I don't know if rushing or not finishing my commitment to the time allotted is worth it.

Not getting through a meditation practice or being interrupted is a common occurrence, not just for single mothers, but for everyone. Distractions are common during meditation and can actually be helpful. So, what is the best way to deal with distractions that unexpectedly come your way during meditation? Does that mother tell her child she's busy, or does she talk to the child and resume later? When she resumes, does she have six minutes to go, or should she start the whole ten minutes again? If I am at work, should I accept a conference meeting

WebEx that just got put on my schedule and delay my meditation until lunch? How can I tell my boss and co-workers that I meditate at a particular time and can't attend the call or meeting?

In most meditation sessions, you will experience internal or external distractions, personal or professional. These distractions should be acknowledged and handled based on sound judgment at the time. Expectations must be set with work and family, and you must let them know you have allotted this specific time every day for the practice. Of course, certain things take precedence, but you must let others know meditation is a priority for your health and well-being. Establishing these boundaries may take juggling time slots for a while, but believe me, everyone will get the message.

When you meditate, planning an activity for your child that you know will keep their attention might be a good idea. If they interrupt, you can ask them to join you in quiet time. During this time (if it works) or with any distraction that took you away from your meditation, gently guide your attention back to your practice. Learning how to manage through distraction is part of the learning process, but with preparation and set expectations, you will command that time for yourself.

Here are some additional tips that can help you.

1. *Set a time expectation where you are unavailable; under most circumstances, you should keep this the same.*

2. *Plan for emergencies or urgent events before your time slot.*

3. *Turn off all cell phones, televisions, computers, or anything that beeps.*

4. *Learn to acknowledge the distraction in your mind, letting it leave slowly as you return to your meditative state.*

5. *If you only get in a limited amount of time and not the full ten minutes, you still have benefited from the experience.*

A significant factor in this is setting boundaries for the practice and relaxing your body and mind no matter where it goes. Your meditation guide can help with this; believe me, it improves with practice.

DEALING WITH A STRESSFUL EPISODE

Stressful episodes are other considerations to work through during meditation. As you read John's meditation focus challenge, clearing the mind clutter should be relatable to anyone who has attempted or is regular to a meditation practice.

John sits down to meditate in his relaxed, high-rise penthouse suite. He has an audio of the sound of wind chimes, and he has set his attention to just relax and focus on the sound of the wind chimes for ten minutes.

One minute into his ten minutes of meditation, his mind loses focus and cannot shake the anxiety that comes from the disagreement he had with his parents. He begins to mentally replay argument after argument that he has been having with his parents. He tries to focus back on the wind chimes, but he cannot block out the visuals of his parent's disapproval of what he wants to do. At this point, he wasn't sure if he should allow his meditation to take place or let this mental interruption win.

John's situation is not unfamiliar. Stressful situations are a constant part of our lives, but how we deal with these trials and tribulations is what matters. The art of meditation is designed to help us manage through these stresses so that we can find that place of calm. By doing this, we are going through what some call mental healing, taking us to better places of resolve. It takes practice, but continuing through the challenging thoughts that come into your head, like John's, results in the beginning of the healing process. When these stressors surface, it's essential to acknowledge them. This simple act of recognition can be empowering. Then gently bring your mind back to that sacred word, mantra, prayer, guided voice, chime, breath, or whatever meditation technique you have chosen. This technique may help you, or you can take part in different meditation and environments or investigate situational meditations that specifically work with your particular needs.

Environmental Concerns

One factor we often hear about is that a person's environment significantly contributes to their practice. We are often asked where we should do it. One person wrote:

"I am just not sure where to meditate. Should I take breaks in the car . . . go into a room in the library . . . take a walk to the park . . . or close my office or bedroom door?"

The answer to those questions is that anywhere safe and comfortable for you is an excellent place to practice. Remember, meditation is being present in the moment, so you can do this by walking your dog or sitting with your eyes closed at your desk. There is no time limit, and studies show that less than ten minutes a day show improved health benefits. No matter where you are, there could be distractions, and you won't be able to create that perfect ambiance at all times. Being in an environment that may seem less than perfect actually increases your practice in that it challenges you to push through the thoughts and distractions to find your place of peace. It is all about conditioning your mind to get past distractions or events that trouble you. So, if you have that terrible day at work that started at 10 a.m., you should take a break to re-group through your meditative practice as soon as time permits, enabling you to find that special place no matter where you are.

You may also want to go through this meditative experience alone, with a group, or through a combination. It is nice to start with a meditation coach or team, as it creates a forum to share your experience. Someone else has experienced many of the things you are experiencing at this early stage, and it helps to talk through these things so that you can break through any barriers preventing you from fully benefiting from the practice. Setting a location or place of calm for yourself during your meditation is essential. Some use candles, oils, incense, and labyrinths, all of which create the right setting for your practice. Experiment with this individually and in groups, and try to cultivate that experience wherever you practice. Remember that meditation is patience in training. To commit to connecting takes patience and persistence. Athletes don't get strong overnight, and it's okay if you don't either. Here are tips for overcoming environmental constraints.

- Decide how long and where you're going to practice.
- Meditate at a particular time, so be in the moment no matter where it is.
- Practice in different settings to build self-awareness and reflection.
- Learn and grow from each distraction and experience.

MEDITATIVE TECHNIQUES

One helpful thing is the use of differing meditative techniques. There is a range of options, including sound techniques (mantras), affirmations (focusing on a phrase vital to you), music (natural or soothing sounds, bells, chimes, singing bowls, etc.), visualization (personal images or places), and movement (yoga, dance, or walking). An example is the use of personal mantras, which are positive phrases or affirmative statements that you say to yourself for motivation or encouragement. This mantra could be your favorite quote, proverb, spiritual truth, or religious saying that motivates and inspires you.

Below are some examples.

> "Ask for what you want and be prepared to get it." —Maya Angelou

> "Excellence does not require perfection."—Henry James

> "Don't put a question mark where God has put a period." —Joel Osteen (via Kim)

SUMMARY

Prepare your meditation section by reviewing the change model, identifying a good environment, and choosing a technique that piques your interest. It is vital that you also work on body awareness. A good meditation coach can help you with breathing, energy flow, and focus and can help guide you to a relaxing state. There are many ways to access coaches and training in meditation, each offering a unique approach. An excellent place to start is a yoga center or place or place where people specialize in holistic training.

Once you have found a coach, you will see that the cost varies. Some sessions are free with an add-on to other services. These are nominal in price and often contain a series of trainings that teach a specific type or style. Elite gyms and community centers are now offering meditation, so it is easy to find qualified coaches in your area. Lastly, the Internet, YouTube, podcasts, blogs, and phone apps are great ways to find qualified meditation experts who can take you through a meditation routine that can be done in person or online.

Meditation aims to open one's mind to any occurring thought, sensation, or emotion and consequently expands the consciousness to a place where one reaches clarity. You may not know this, but most people have created this place for themselves. That's why we know the difference between happiness and unhappiness. Through meditation, you can imagine being in that place at any time, allowing your body, mind, and soul to have time for you. You will be surprised at the answers to questions, creativity, healing, and clarity all gained from this all-encompassing gift.

Chapter 8: Grounding Yourself for a Successful Meditative Practice

LEARNING TO GROUND YOURSELF FOR SUCCESS

APPROACHING A SUCCESSFUL MEDITATIVE practice starts with grounding yourself. A primary goal of meditation is to create change. Inability to change our behaviors and outcomes is partly due to our fear of failure and our continual attachment to something or someone. The need is to focus more on what we are wanting to experience, because many distractions pull us and cloud our thoughts. We are rarely in a present state of awareness. Meditation changes this, as it helps us focus. This allows us to grow and change by eliminating the clutter and being present in the moment. People can change when they are self-aware, receive support, and become intentional about behaving differently. But this change in mindset takes time, which sometimes feels challenging.

The *Chavous/Chavous-Kambach GROUND model* contains process steps that can help you have a better meditation practice. These *six steps to change* prepare you to:

1. *Get acclimated to your environment*
2. *Realize your vision*
3. *Open your mental capacity*
4. *Use meditation to increase inner strength*
5. *Notice the wins and conflicts*
6. *Dedicate yourself to effective and continual renewal*

This change model starts with the foundation of awareness, realization, and openness, and then continues on to use, noticing, and dedication. In any meditation practice, grounding yourself will help you reach your desired state of calm and give you a more focused intention for the practice.

G—Get acclimated to your environment

R—Realize your vision

O—Open your mental capacity

U—se meditation to increase inner strength

N—otice wins and conflicts

D—edicate yourself to continual change and renewal

GET ACCLIMATED TO YOUR ENVIRONMENT

Get Acclimated—The major environmental factors influencing meditation are time, place, space, climate, and noise. Before you begin your meditation practice, work to identify potential factors that might come into play. Remove the ones in your control: close the window, shut the door, and silence the cell phone. For those you can't control, remember to acknowledge, accept, and release it any time it enters your practice.

1. *Acknowledging means admitting the existence or truth of the distraction or thought that you are presented with.*

2. *Accepting means consenting to receive the distraction or thought.*

3. *Releasing means letting the distraction or thought go and flow freely out of your mind and focus.*

Remember, a successful practice involves not only preparing but also acclimating yourself to the environment. It involves adjusting oneself to it gradually, no matter what condition or distraction presents itself. Meditation can be practiced in all environments; it just takes creating your personal space despite any circumstance. The key is not letting the environment limit you or the practice you want to experience.

Guide Tips:

1. **Remember, meditation is not a judgmental practice.** *Only concern yourself with awareness of the environment, but not with it being a pitfall to a successful practice.*

2. **Most of what we recall during a meditation practice is a recent thought.** *Processing current thoughts is a normal process. A good best practice is to go over and bring awareness before the practice so you can move freely into a practice state.*

3. **Stay attentive to the practice and remind yourself that you are meditating.** *When a distractive moment occurs, it is expected that you get sidetracked. Don't let it stop you from enjoying the moment; rather, begin to refocus, bringing yourself back to the present.*

4. **Refocus on the problems that occur in your practice.** *It is up to you to bring the correct refocusing back to your practice. If it is a posture problem, re-adjust; if you are in pain, engage in diaphragmatic (deep) breathing and speak to yourself in positive acceptance. This refocus on the problems occurring in practice can be difficult depending on*

the situation, but controlling the moment takes time. Do things only to the best of your ability and nothing more.

Contemplation:

Develop a mantra, scripture, affirmation, or focus reminder that will bring your attention back to your meditation session and help you acclimate to your ideal environment.

....

....

....

REALIZE YOUR VISION

Realize your Vision—Most people do not visualize where they want their practice to take them. Nothing is wrong with this, as the primary goal of meditation is to go beyond the mind to a state of happiness and bliss. For us, that state of bliss is our faith. For you, it may be different. Regardless, if the mind and its clutter are an obstacle to finding your bliss, setting a vision and intentions can enhance your practice by helping you process the clutter and create the desired experiences. This state of bliss can be accomplished by establishing a vision that is a place of calm for you. This vision needs to be real and personal, and you should engage in and connect to this place so that your senses respond to it. Realization can be accomplished through affirmations, spot checks, and reminders that support it.

Guide Tips:

1. *Be specific in your vision or intention. The best way to give your intention or vision value is to be specific. This specificity should embrace your dreams and goals, giving them absolute power.*

2. *Manifest what your vision looks like. A vision defines your optimal desired state in the future state. It tells you what to achieve and gives you the why. Work to define your dreams so they manifest both internally and externally.*

3. *Develop affirmations that support it. Choose an affirmation that works for you. Remember that conscious thoughts support you. Your vision or affirmation should focus on you having what you want and how it looks in the present moment.*

4. *Have a spirit of gratitude. Consistent gratitude will amplify your life and focus, and your vision will flourish. Get out of your old mindset and walk in a new, mindful presence.*

Contemplation:

Write down your vision, intention for your meditation, and an affirmation that focuses on what you want to manifest. Know that this could change depending on the practice.

....

....

....

OPEN YOUR MENTAL CAPACITY

Open your mental capacity—When your mind thrives, you do, too. Meditation has been shown to preserve the brain's gray matter by decreasing its loss, which is the cause of stress and declining health. You can preserve your brain by opening your mind's capacity to do so and focusing on that intention. Know that opening your mental capacity through meditation helps you become more focused and less worried about discomfort. In the process, you can begin to gain a better understanding of how to control the clutter in your mind and become more appreciative of things life offers you. Meditative practice helps you form habits and opens you to awareness, choices, and freedom.

Guide Tips:

Develop a routine and habit for brain health. Daily meditation improves total well-being. It relieves anxiety and depression and improves attention and concentration. Establish this habit for overall psychological well-being.

Perform a daily check-in with yourself. Opening your mind takes daily check-ins with yourself. This is not only a best practice, but making this a regular routine trains the mind to notice. Before you dive into anything, take a few moments to check in with yourself and others.

Heart-centered practices involve quieting the mind. A skill we are rarely taught is listening. Meditation allows us time to quiet our minds, enabling us to listen to all aspects of our being. Allow yourself to experience the mental, physical, and spiritual aspects of being still.

Get to know yourself through learning and training. The practice of meditation isn't just about focusing or emptying your mind. It's about learning how your mind works, what's in and should be, and ultimately, putting the right things in the right place. That's when the actual healing starts, and the learning process begins.

Contemplation:

How will you be still and perform daily check-ins with yourself to uncover your feelings or triggers that are affecting your health?

....

....

....

....

USE YOUR INNER STRENGTH TO MAKE CHANGE

Use Meditation to increase your inner strength— You possess the innate inner fortitude to create a powerful meditative practice. As you live in your committed practice, you will be a model for others, as it will be visible in all you do. Acknowledge your change when others notice and let it propel you along the way. Use your meditative practice for continual growth and development for yourself and to support others. Although inner strength comes from within, we sometimes don't realize the power of our strength until we dig deep into ourselves. Some specific traits and concepts typically make up inner strength, but the acknowledgment of these is in our acceptance that all seasons in life are meaningful. We must learn to draw from our strengths in these seasons, and the practice of Meditation helps us do this.

Guide Tips:

1. **Acknowledge your change for continued growth.** *This acknowledgment requires you to use the capacity required to recognize something about the new you. You then must own it and celebrate the groundbreaking change it has made within you.*

2. **Model the behavior and be aware of how it affects others.** *As you become*

> *aware of your inner strength, use it to*
> *model behavior for others. Replace stress*
> *for calm and weakness for strength.*
> *Be quick to hear, slow to speak, and*
> *slow to anger.*

3. **Give rise to the Atma Bala**—*the*
   strength of the soul. Your inner strength
   is your core, and the strength of the soul
   comes through faith and obedience.

4. **Become your own best friend.** *Enjoy*
   spending time with yourself and watching
   the noticeable progress you make. The
   breakthroughs come from emotional intel-
   ligence, like seeing and congratulating
   yourself often.

Contemplation:

How will you use the inner strength found through
Meditation to support life seasons, growth, and
development?

....

....

....

....

....

....

....

NOTICE THE SMALL AND BIG WINS AND WHAT PREVENTS YOUR VISION

Notice and be aware of wins and conflicts. Understand your stressors and the things that prevent you from reaching a place of calm. Regardless of the source, take time to remove them from your life or control their effects on you. After incorporating this awareness and attention into your daily routine, you will be better able to calm yourself when faced with any challenge. As you experience the benefits resulting from this, acknowledge your success. Notice and be aware of wins and conflicts in your meditation practice. Life should not be taken for granted, nor should one give in to conflict. Extend well wishes that include compassion, kindness, appreciation, honoring, cherishing, and love. Celebrate your life and the lives of others.

Guide Tips:

1. **Utilize Body scans in your practice.** *An important part of any meditative practice is using body scans to bring awareness to wholeness. It helps with thoughts, emotions, and physical sensations, resulting in heightened awareness and confidence.*

2. **Start your day, but don't let it start you.** *Starting your day is a great way to set a positive routine for the day. It*

helps to support a good day and helps
to overcome challenges should it not go
so well. Although you may experience a
challenge that is hard to overcome, using
this routine daily will ensure a good day
most of the time.

3. **Understand your stressors.** *We all*
    have a breaking point and can be thrown
    into fight-or-flight for different reasons.
    The key is to know what triggers you
    into a stressful state and work on ways to
    counteract it.

4. **Face conflict.** *Many people find it dif-*
    ficult to handle conflict. In the Kilmann
    conflict resolution theory, avoiding,
    compromising, accommodating, and
    collaborating can be used to overcome it.
    Mediation can also be used in conflict
    resolution, as conflict starts from within.
    Meditation helps one approach a behav-
    ior change, creating a positive outcome
    for everyone.

Contemplation:

How will you celebrate yourself and your wins and overcome conflict?

....

....

DEDICATE YOURSELF TO EFFECTIVE AND CONTINUAL CHANGE

Dedicate yourself to effective and continual renewal—Change is good and renewal is too! You will experience change and renewal as you dedicate yourself to your meditation practice. It takes consistency to see continual results. This means making it a priority in your life and committing to a daily meditation routine. Renewal is the act of being made new, fresh, or strong again, and this is accomplished by being wholly entrenched in your meditative practice. It takes setting an enthusiastic agreement with yourself. If meditation is practiced regularly and you have dedicated yourself to it, the renewal process will be automatic and sustainable.

Guide Tips:

1. **Establish a meditation routine.**
   Studies have shown that meditating for only ten minutes a day is all you need to experience positive benefits. Set a daily routine so you will experience continued success.

2. **Assess and reassess your goals and vision.** *Vision and goals change. One value of meditation is how well one navigates through these changes, maintaining clarity and focus. Meditation is*

*a successful tool in emotional intelligence
and sustaining positive change.*

3. **Continue to implement and act on
   areas of difficulty.** *Meditation improves
   the mind, body, and heart. Its relaxation
   response helps in all areas of well-being.
   Each person has a personally challenging
   area of life. Addressing this area with
   more effort, focus, and support is important. This awareness can be achieved
   through meditation or other traditional
   and non-traditional practices.*

Pay it forward to others: This is asking someone
to repay your kindness by doing a good deed for
someone else. This helps you earn trust and inspires
generosity and compassion. It helps us with the dedication and renewal area as we focus on the broader
concept of kindness for ourselves and others.

Contemplation:

How will you sustain the renewal process?

....

....

....

....

....

....

....

....

Chapter 9: The Situational Meditation Journal

SITUATIONAL MEDITATION **IS ABOUT** finding this space and learning to engage in contemplation or reflection. It helps you regain focus on the essential things in life and manage those pressing issues clouding your mind. In short, situational meditation means designing your routine to take on whatever significance you want in your life, whether health and wellness, faith-based, or otherwise.

Meditation, as a practice, trains your mind to focus better on life and its purpose. Once you begin only a few minutes a day of this training, you start to realize the change in your mindset. You would also be surprised to know that meditation takes more commitment than time, so all that is needed is a ritual set toward the practice.

In the Situation Meditation Journal, we will briefly introduce the history, origin, and benefits of the common forms of meditation found in this book, helping you build a strong foundation in meditation. *The journal includes twelve daily activities and two days for recovery.* The twelve days are purposefully designed for reflection, healing, and awareness integral to your journey toward peace and transformation. The seventh and fourteenth days are dedicated to Recap, Repeat, Reflect, and Recover, providing a weekly summary of your healing progress. Journaling is a form of meditation that brings consciousness and awareness of areas of yourself and your life. It enlightens you with the knowledge of what needs to change and how to affect those changes.

This *Situational Meditation* book, along with the *GROUND Change Model*, are your comprehensive guides to starting a meditation journey. The book delves into the theory and practice of meditation, providing a deep understanding of its healing properties and how it can support your mental and emotional well-being. The *GROUND Change Model*, on the other hand, is a practical framework that helps you apply the principles of meditation to your daily life, fostering self-awareness and transformation. Understanding the art form's past and present practices is essential for readers, and enables them to make informed decisions and appropriate choices for their meditation practice.

Chapter 10: Real Life Meditation Stories

"Life to me is love, fun, interactive, and a meditative experience in the stages of one's life."

—Natalia Cota-Kambach (12 years old)

IN THIS SECTION OF Situational Meditation, we will share stories of how meditation, with its profound and transformative power, has helped resolve some of life's most stressful situations. Hearing how different stressors affect others and how individuals are overcoming them through meditation is a good way to understand the benefits of meditation.

We have also found that because many people want to meditate and are looking for a guide, technique, or explanation that helps them get started, sharing real stories from real people could be deeply relatable to what you are going through or see in others, enabling you to find a path of healing that resonates with your unique journey.

We hope you read these stories and learn that starting a meditation practice can be a simple yet powerful tool to help you cope more effectively with your situation. The profound effects of meditation are not reserved for a select few, but can be experienced by anyone who is willing to start. No matter how difficult the situation or goal, meditation can make a difference.

We always say life happens, and despite our difficulties, we must strive to find peace with it all, if not in others, then in ourselves. Stories like these are a testimony to overcoming stress and crises. Through the stories of people like you, we can witness how to turn our attention from the flood of anxious thoughts that overwhelmed us to just a few minutes of focused situational meditation, helping us address anxious thoughts positively. We will always have stress, but how we respond to and control it is essential.

CANDICE'S MOVING STORY

Many of us are nesters, needing to feel assured of the security and safety of our homes. It is important to remember that you're not alone in this experience of feeling stress during a move. According to a 2021 Zillow study, more than half (55 percent) of individuals experiencing a move reported feeling stress, and 48 percent claimed to have anxiety during relocation. These feelings are common, whether your move is exciting or challenging. The stress-related symptoms, such as insomnia, oversleeping, head-aches, fatigue, and changes in eating habits are all part of the process.

Moving, whether caused by good or bad circum-stances, can be a disruptive change. However, it also holds the potential for positive transformation. Candice's story shows how, even during heightened times of stress, maintaining a regular routine like meditation can be a powerful tool for managing the challenges of a move.

It was only two days before Candice's big move, so she had gotten up early to review her last-minute checklist. She was fortunate to have a moving company pack and unpack their belongings, but even with that, she wanted to ensure things were in place for the move. Usually, Candice would be off to her regular daily situational meditation routine, which incorporated a long contemplative walk and focused gym workout. But today, she decided to follow what she had done for the past two weeks and pass on everything except the task at hand. She went to her desk to review the long, dreaded list before her, and although things looked in place, she felt an overwhelming feeling that something was missing. She started feeling anxious, something she hadn't felt in months.

Candice tried to work through the feeling, but an enor-mous sense of fear overcame her.

"What are we doing? We were leaving our friends, family, and routines, all for a career opportunity we weren't sure of!"

Her thoughts began to race further as she affirmed her agreement with her husband to take advantage of the move out of California to a promotional opportunity in New Mexico.

Lower cost of living, beautiful sunsets, and activities like hiking, skiing, and exploring national parks, which we both loved to do. Not to mention we have a renter for our home, but is this the right thing to do? What if they don't pay, or we can't find a job to bring us back if we hate it?

Beads of sweat dampened Candice's forehead, and her heart began to race. She felt like she couldn't breathe, and her heart started to race with anxiety.

Her phone rang, and it was her friend Eugenia. Eugenia could immediately tell by Candice's voice that she wasn't quite right. Before Candice could talk, Eugenia began to ask her to walk her through a breathing exercise they had practiced on their situational walks. Candice followed her through a guided meditation session on the phone. Through the breaths, Candice began to experience the fantastic release and calm, and she began to relax a bit as she listened to Eugenia guide her to that calm place. With each remembrance of thoughts to the move, Eugenia reminded her to acknowledge, accept, and release that thought and bring her attention back to the breaths. As Candice let go of the things that did not serve her, she began to release those things that came to mind. She acknowledged the thought, released it, and returned to her breath. When her mind drifted, she returned to her breath and felt her special, calm place.

Her mind went to her favorite corner in her room, where she would light her sacred candle and incense to begin her practice, and then to the situational walk, where she leisurely contemplated the scenery. *Interestingly, she could imagine all of this with her phone in her ear. Eugenia went on for ten minutes, and then they sat in silence for five.*

As lovely bells rang, taking them out of the profound peace of their meditation, Candice was thankful for the session, friendship, and the peace she was given. She felt a profound sense of relief. "What would I do without you, Eugenia?" Candice asked. Eugenia replied, "Just like we did today . . . breathe." Three months passed, and Candice was now in her new home. That day taught her that distance does not affect fellowship; you can create your place of calm anywhere and be disciplined in your meditation practice, especially during stressful times.

Juliana's Bullying Story

Bullying has become an epidemic in American society. It is defined as unwanted, aggressive behavior among school-aged children involving a real or perceived power imbalance. Countless studies have shown improvements in health-related effects like behavioral conditions through implementing sitting-meditative practices among youth aged six to eighteen in schools, clinics, and community settings across all meditation modalities, including mindfulness meditation, transcendental meditation, mindfulness-based stress reduction, and mindfulness-based cognitive therapy. Outreach and awareness campaigns for victims of bullying can increase self-worth and, more importantly, save lives. Juliana's story should raise awareness of this problem and also give victims of bullying a place where they can find support externally and within themselves.

Juliana was six when she was brought to this country from overseas. Her parents immigrated to the US under the worst of conditions. The only English she knew was what she heard on TV or through a passing American who sounded foreign. Her Spanish and IQ were great, but she was pushed further and further behind in school due to her inexperience with the English language. To complicate things even more, her classmates would do mean things to her— eating her lunch, asking her to give up her chair, taking her belongings, and continuously chanting harsh words and threats. Her parents would console her but would tell her to work to get along and fit in, not knowing the seriousness of bullying problems in schools.

One day, an unexpected, life-changing event happened—a substitute teacher, Ms. Wells, filled in for her regular teacher. Juliana felt a real connection to her, as did the other children, even the troubled ones. On day two of her filling in with Juliana's class, she announced that she had gotten approval from the parents and school district to conduct a pilot program that involved the class participating in quiet time for ten minutes. There wasn't much protest because ten minutes away from coursework is welcomed by kids in most classrooms. The program lasted three months, and although Juliana's regular teacher returned, Ms. Wells still conducted the ten-minute sessions throughout the time allotted.

Those three months were a turning point not just for Juliana but also for her bullies. The class may not have noticed it at first, but a peaceful calm permeated the students and everyone who participated in the quiet time. The atmosphere became less hostile, more tolerant, and less fraught with anger. The pilot program's success was so profound that it continued long after Ms. Wells's departure, leaving a lasting legacy of positivity. The long-term effects of this intervention are evident in Juliana's continued success, and the improved classroom environment. Juliana's transformation is nothing short of a miracle. She is now a high school honor student, fluent in English, well-liked by her peers, and a dedicated daily meditation practitioner. She often wonders where she would be today without the life-changing

experience with Ms. Wells. The impact of that inter-
vention is undeniable, and it serves as a beacon of hope
for all those struggling with similar challenges.

RIA'S SELF-IMAGE AND BEING A TEEN STORY

If you have any interaction with kids (or if you have gone through puberty yourself), you know how puberty affects teenagers physically and emotionally. They are concerned with the perfect body image, how they are perceived, and how to fit in with their peers. Encouraging children to be physically active and engage in activities for fun and physical health can help them to appreciate what their body can do, rather than focusing on their body's appearance. Ria's story shows how attending a yoga class helped her through some of the experiences she was going through as a teen.

Ria didn't know what happened to her this year, but she woke up one morning not knowing who that other person was she was looking at in the mirror. She had felt so self-confident before, but did not like what she saw or felt at that moment. She was trying to understand who this person was and get control of her emotional hormones. She felt judged by her friends and misunderstood by her parents. All the pressures of being like the images in magazines, television, and social media were stressful, and she felt out of control.

Sara, one of her friends, attended a yoga class at one of the centers near her home. As with teenagers, they all began noticing her change after her three-month practice. She was calmer, less concerned with what others or her friends thought, and had started to build a unique look for herself. She was more focused and seemed more engaged.

Ria asked if she could attend a few classes with Sara. At first, she felt intimidated, but then the experience overwhelmed her and created a transformation that she began to love. She was still hormonal and sometimes affected by her peers' thoughts, but she, like Sara, was beginning to transform both in mind and body.

KEITH AND SUSAN'S DIVORCE STORY

Divorce is a significant stressor that affects us in more ways than we think. Gallup reported that 44.1 percent of divorced Americans experienced anxiety, compared to only 38.6 percent of married respondents who reported being stressed. Of particular importance is the fact that more separated women felt stressed compared to women who had divorced. In addition to the family impact, it can also affect our finances and our mental and emotional well-being. Family turmoil can cause chronic damage to relationships and can leave permanent scars. The story below shows how a family vacation to a Buddhist retreat had a profound impact on this family's lives.

It was inevitably going to happen . . . Keith and I were divorcing. Our arguments and problems had gotten more intense, and even the counselors had succumbed to divorce being a reality and the best thing for us. The sad part was that we were both husband and wife and friends who shared two wonderful children. The strain of our marital problems had become so severe that it began affecting the kids, family, and friends. Even Keith's work was comprised, resulting in fewer sales and diminished commission, which he had consistently brought into the household. We filed for divorce, which was finalized quickly because we both agreed to a fair and equitable split.

After the split, things were similar. There was this awkwardness in our family that created a space between us. Looking at the vacation card in my hand, I remembered how we had gotten it. Before the divorce, we had attended a Buddhist temple with a family friend. We weren't members of any religion, so the experience of attending was actually good for us. The temple was giving away a trip to a meditation retreat, and our family won. But that was then, and this is now. Even though it was free and a planned trip, now we were at a different place in our family life, which diminished our enthusiasm for attending. However, after much discussion, we agreed that maybe one last trip as a family might be a good thing, so we headed from Colorado to Washington for this so-called family vacation.

The retreat was all-inclusive, and we had to follow the itinerary. The schedule revolved around family programs, but each had an individual focus. They practiced mindfulness meditation several times a day, and we learned techniques that helped hone in on the skill. We participated in prayers for world peace, and the activities were geared around the ages of our children and how to develop a happy and peaceful mind. We were there for a week and were changed. The distance we had felt from the divorce disappeared. We could talk and not fight, and our kids began communicating with us again. We have since gone every year and are now practicing mindfulness meditation daily. Although we have not remarried, the relationship that we have now as a family is even better than it was before, and Keith's income has tripled. Meditation changed not only my life but also the lives of my entire family.

COLIN'S WORKFORCE/WORK-LIFE BALANCE STORY

Problems at work can affect our home life. If we are unhappy, these problems can create a river that spills into our personal lives, drowning us and those around us. Many problems with work-life balance have to do with us not being able to separate these two very distinct areas of our lives. This work-life balance issue is compounded when these problems have to do with the stability of our homes and the lives we have established for ourselves and our families. Colin, a very successful designer, tells how centering prayer and meditation brought him back to a focus that was free from worry and re-established the separation between work and home.

Colin was in a company of constant flux. His company had been purchased several times, and he wasn't sure from day to day what that meant for him. He was a strong Christian but felt he was losing his personal experience with Christ due to his preoccupied mind. The changes in leadership, condition, and possible employment consumed his thoughts. At lunch with a colleague, he expressed frustration with his job and mentality. He was never good with change, but this company seemed to be playing a game of Russian roulette in his life. It affected his work and home life, and he couldn't separate them. He just wanted to stop for a moment and think again.

James listened intently and suggested that Colin read up on centering prayer. It is a form of meditation and prayer designed to bring a person closer to Christ. James started going two years ago, and it changed his relationship with God and gave him more clarity and focus at work, resulting in a recent promotion. Colin noticed the difference in him, and so did others. Colin agreed to attend the centering prayer meeting with James during their lunch breaks the following week.

On the day he attended, the leader went over what to expect, what to do, and the basic premise of the practice.

He and the others began with silence for twenty minutes, focusing on a sacred word. As he began to work to focus, tons of thoughts came to his mind. He had been told that this was normal and, as instructed, returned his thoughts to the sacred word. His first experience with centering prayer was challenging, sitting in silence for that long, but then it became something he longed for. When the time came for the session to end, he felt he didn't have enough time.

As a result of his centering prayer experience, his focus and attitude changed, and a few of his colleagues noticed and even mentioned this to him. He sat with James at lunch and thanked him for the experience, hoping that he would be able to help share this experience with others. James was no longer worried about tomorrow, but became more thankful each day.

MICHELLE'S DEATH IN THE FAMILY STORY

Death is part of life, but the death of a loved one is something that causes significant stress. We grieve for our loved ones, and our lives can become permanently seriously disrupted. Meditation can help you observe your thoughts and feelings without getting swept away by them, making the intense emotions more manageable. It can also help reduce stress and anxiety, which often accompany grief, by focusing your mind and bringing you into the present moment. Michelle tells a story of how meditation helped her deal with the loss of her mother.

I was driving home one night, crying my eyes out. I had been so not myself, and the cold, dreary day in Indiana didn't help. I realize that death is a part of life, but I wanted to do so many things with my mom that I wasn't able to do. It had started to snow, and the snow began to stick to the trees, which meant the expected snowstorm was here. I was minutes away from home, which I was thankful for. It looked like tomorrow would be a snow day, which was nice since I was so sad and heavy with grief. I pulled into the garage and went inside. In the mirror, I saw how bad I looked. I kept thinking that I hoped I didn't look this bad in front of my peers and co-workers and that it was no wonder people seemed to be avoiding me.

My home was my castle, and everything was beautiful, just like I had worked so hard to create, but even that didn't help. I would give it all up for one more day with my mom. I turned the radio on and off, hating the music, and went into the kitchen to look at my mail. In the stack was a flash drive from "The Guided Meditation Experts" that asked me to try this free introductory session.

I went to my computer and opened up the drive to listen. It had the most calming nature sounds, and the woman's voice was relaxing. She took me to places in the woods that connected me to my mom, who loved hiking with me. At one point, I felt that she was walking alongside me as we watched the owl in the highest tree limb and the deer grazing in the grass. I imagined seeing her jump when the brush started moving, laughing when it was just a group of rabbits running for protection from something bigger than them.

When the session ended, I felt like I had experienced meditation and time with my mom. I slept like a baby and, for the first time, actually had a dream that I remember! I enrolled to get several of their CDs, downloaded them, and now listen to them religiously every night. I will say that there is not a day that I don't miss my mom, but the visualization and messages I get from the meditation tell me she is always with me.

KARA'S DATING STORY

A relationship of any kind takes work. The best relationships can bring joy and contentment, but at their worst, they can cause stress and pain. Kara's story tells how meditation can aid in the healing process. Kara used meditation to soothe and conquer her pain that resulted from an unsuccessful relationship.

Kara was in a relationship with manipulation and anger as its primary components. Her relationship ended abruptly, and soon after, she began to feel worn down and stressed because she missed the relationship. Kara loved animals and usually found peace with them. She was distraught after the breakup and decided to try to redirect herself by meditation with a focus on the animals that she loved.

Every day got more manageable, but she still longed to call her ex regularly. Whenever she thought of calling, she would take two to five minutes to close her eyes and meditate. She would start by thinking of her little pup, "Tiger," who was, in her eyes, her power animal. Then, she would focus on the word heal. Sometimes, she would cry when the thoughts and words would enter her mind, but it was all part of the healing process, and she was able to refrain from making a phone call or text.

After ten days, she felt that she had more control and was able to get her life on track. By fifteen days, she felt she was able to enjoy things with friends without thinking of her ex too often and was able to ignore his calls. By thirty days, she felt like she did before meeting him. Allowing time to mourn the relationship and heal with meditation was critical to her process.

As you can see, we all have stories, each resonating differently. Stories, with their power to build empathy, connect us to a narrative that is more significant and more personal than our world view. In meditation, storytelling can help with visualization, reflection, empathy, knowledge, inspiration, and therapeutic processes in some situations. The stories we shared were experienced by people like you and me, who benefited by being in the moment and letting go of their powerful voices to heal themselves and others. Storytelling allows us to inspire and captivate, invites conversation, inspires the imagination, and captures hearts.

We must continue to share stories as they create an emotional connection. This helps us understand each other and gain a deeper connection to our experiences. As you recall, one of the areas in our *GROUND* change model was noticing and being aware of wins and conflicts. Regardless of the source of our pain, we must take the time to remove life conflicts and celebrate our successes. Understand your stressors and what prevents you from reaching a calm place. Regardless of the source, take time to remove them from your life or control their effects on you. Celebrate your life and the lives of others. We share these stories as wins, acknowledging and valuing each participant's journey! As seasoned meditation practitioners, we've noticed that many people are eager to meditate but often need a guide, technique, or explanation to get started. The *Situational Meditation Journal* is a guide providing an interactive journal to start or enhance your mindful meditation transformational journey. It serves as a companion to this theoretical book, helping you put the theory you've learned into practice. The journal encourages you to adopt a situational meditation approach, free from rules or boundaries, fostering self-love and transformation. It is designed to inspire and motivate you with the transformative power of meditation.

Purchase a *Situational Meditation Journal* online or at your local bookstore.

Continued Research

WE ARE LOOKING TO expand our field of research and understand how the G.R.O.U.N.D. change guide has worked in your lives. Our research will involve formulating a book with real-world experiences of those who have used the Chavous/Chavous-Kambach G.R.O.U.N.D. Guide. If you want to be in the book, please jot down your experiences and contact us for more details.

Looking to get started in meditation? Strategic Ladies can help.

Strategic Ladies wants their readers to know that they are here to support them with any additional information, research, and practical application of meditation. We can provide information on our program offerings, additional meditative practices, and resources that are available. Our wide variety of services include workshops, speaker events, consulting, and research.

Contact us at office@strategicladies.com
Email: Office@strategicladies.com
Website: www.strategicladies.com

About the Authors

STRATEGIC LADIES BELIEVE THAT you can grow by harnessing the power within you and identifying where you are in the three selves. The process involves resolving inner conflicts and aligning the three selves before entering into each Situational Meditation practice. This understanding empowers you, instilling confidence and self-assurance in your journey of personal growth.

(1) The first is the *Fighting Self*, the inner voice that often undermines our confidence and diminishes our power. It's the self that we need to recognize and overcome.

(2) The second is the *Acknowledging Self*, the point at which one accepts oneself and gains an understanding of oneself.

(3) The last is the *Chosen Self*, where one harnesses the above powers to reach the desired self.

Our Manifesto is not just a *plan of action* but rather a *call to action* to just being. Knowing that each person's fights, acknowledgments, and chosen paths are different makes each person's Manifesto uniquely beautiful and personal. We each have one; it takes harnessing the power within to release it.

ABOUT DR. ESTELLA

Dr. Estella Chavous is an experienced educator, communicator, global marketer, and wellbeing consultant. Estella has significant professional experience in education, sales, and marketing, working in strategic leadership positions for Fortune 500 companies, including Abbott, Amgen, Bristol Myers-Squibb, and Schneider-Electric. Her marketing and people team experience includes domestic work in the pharmaceutical, biotech, and software industries and global assignments based overseas. She has built and led effective teams throughout her career, designed and implemented successful strategies, and developed and managed diverse programs, ranging from sales and marketing initiatives to employee wellness programs, enabling the transformational process.

Dr. Estella Chavous is deeply committed to education and knowledge sharing. As an Adjunct Professor at *UMass Global and Chandler-Gilbert Community College*, she imparts her wealth of experience and expertise to the next generation of professionals. Her dedication is evident in her teaching of various business, international business, marketing, and professional studies courses. Dr. Estella is

also an Insight Timer Meditation Trainer (https://
insighttimer.com/) and the co-host of Edge God In
(EGI)(https://edgegodin.com/), and the voice of
Emotional Intelligence in Christ (https://emotion-
alintelligenceinchrist.com/) which she co-founded.

Dr. Estella is not just an educator and consultant,
but also a visionary entrepreneur. As a co-owner of
Strategic Ladies and the *Mindful Media* show, she
has demonstrated her leadership and commitment
to the health and well-being of self and others. Her
multifaceted skills are showcased in these ventures,
which focus on making a positive impact. Dr.
Estella has also authored several books, including
*Situational Meditation: A Guide to the Theory and
Practice of Meditation*, the *Situational Meditation
Journal*, a Christ-filled assessment, and a booklet.

ABOUT DR. JAI

Dr. Jacinta Chavous-Kambach (Dr. Jai) is a
best-selling author, magazine columnist, Intuitive
Relationship & Intimacy Coach, speaker, and
diversity advocate. Her passion, experience, and
education allow her to use her skills and gift of intu-
ition in her business and writing.

Dr. Jai holds a Bachelor of Arts in Communication
from *California University San Marcos*, an M.B.A in
Organizational Psychology and Development from
*American Intercontinental University Los Angeles/
London*, and an Educational Doctorate in

Organizational Leadership from *Chapman University System.*

She is the co-host of the Strategic Ladies Mindful Media Show Radio Show, an adjunct professor, and an avid reader and writer. She is the co-author of the bestseller book Situational Meditation: The Theory and Practice of Meditation, which gets to the grit of meditation and how it can positively impact one's life.

Dr. Jai is a published BMI singer and songwriter who has worked with many accomplished artists. She has written with Emmy award-winning songwriter Janie Lidey and has debut singles, I Know You Want Me (https://music.youtube.com/watch?v=tOiEOyUbaTc&list=RDAMVM-tOiEOyUbaTc) and Hyperventilate (https://music.youtube.com/watch?v=Lqw3ZP-wHMM&list=R-DAMVMLqw3ZP-wHMM), co-written with Paul Hines, an award-winning artist who collaborated with Teena Marie, Michael Jackson, and Debarge. She won the title of Ms. Egypt in the Queen of the Universe Pageant 2016, winning the title and trophy of best smile.

Cheeky, intuitive, and free-spirited, Dr. Jai loves life, reading, writing, and connecting with people. She also admits to her love for elephants and antiques.

References

Chavous, Estella. "The Effects of Meditation Treatments in Managing Workforce Stress with Women in Leadership" (Doctor of Ed. Diss., Brandman University, 2015), ProQuest (28497262). https://www.proquest.com/openview/c9747fc0eb2c7e5df84370bf2dcffa3e/1?pq-orig-site=gscholar&cbl=18750&diss=y.

Chavous-Kambach, Jacinta. "The Effects of Music Treatments in Managing Workforce Stress with Women in Leadership" (Doctor of Ed. Diss., Brandman University, 2016), ProQuest (10113234).

https://www.proquest.com/docview/1800807173/abstract/B4D7E0F499D147FFPQ/1?sourcetype=Dissertations%20&%20Theses.